Communication Barriers, Motivational Theories, Sexual Harassment, and Absenteeism in Organizations

4 Topics in 1 Book

Louis Bevoc

Published by
NutriNiche System LLC

Communication Barriers
In Organizations
Understanding, Exemplifying, and Preventing

Louis Bevoc

Published by
NutriNiche System LLC

Introduction

Types

Causes and Prevention

Summary

Introduction

What are barriers to communication? Essentially, they are roadblocks to understanding the meaning of messages sent from sender to receiver. In other words, they hinder communication between people.

In organizations, barriers to communication cause a wealth of problems that decrease workplace efficiency. Misunderstanding prevents tasks from being accomplished, and this hinders the achievement of organizational goals and objectives. When goals are not accomplished, organizations become stagnant...and some even cease to exist.

Workplace communication is influenced by a variety of different factors. Three major factors include:

Noise

Many different kinds of noise create distractions in workplaces. These distractions hinder communication by causing employees to misinterpret messages. Examples include telephones, faxes, coworker conversations, customer visits, interviews, vendor appointments, audits, facility tours, music, and loudspeaker systems.

Hierarchy

Authority has a direct impact on communication. Some employees high up on the corporate ladder do not make an effort to communicate with those on lower rungs. Interestingly, the opposite is also true. Some employees at lower levels do not try to communicate with those in higher positions. This makes absolutely no sense from an organizational communication standpoint, but it does happen quite frequently. These groups think of themselves as distinct, and they only communicate with coworkers on the same level.

Words

Certain words used in workplaces are esoteric. This means they have meaning to people who possess specialized knowledge, but they are confusing to many other individuals. Examples include the following:

Jargon

These are words or expressions used by a particular trade, industry, or profession. They are very specific, and generally not understood by outsiders. Examples include *agonal* (a medical term that shows a turn for the worse in a patient's condition), *code eight* (a law enforcement term that means a police officer needs immediate help), and *trimmed to the blue* (a meat processing term that means all the fat has been removed from a ham).

Acronyms

These are abbreviations that represent words or a phrase. FDA (Food and Drug Administration), CEO (Chief Executive Officer), and YMCA (Young Men's Christian Association) are some common examples that are understood by a fairly wide variety of people. However, the majority of terms in this category are far less familiar...especially those from the military. Examples include NFO (Naval Flight Officer), DFAC (Dining Facility), and BCD (Bad Conduct Discharge).

The above factors influence communication in organizations, and they often create communication barriers. These barriers can be broken down into specific types, and this is done in the next section.

Types

Barriers to communication can be defined by types. Essentially, this means breaking them down into categories for classification and better understanding. The following are some specific types using workplace examples for clarification:

Selective perception

This involves employees who see and hear only what they want to see and hear. They do not consider any opposing, contradictory, or differing viewpoints because they have established a position where change is not an option. This is a barrier to communication because bias results when all viewpoints are not considered.

Organizational example

Tom is the owner of a gym that specializes in strength conditioning. He believes weightlifting is the best exercise for people because they continue to burn calories after their workout.

One day, while reading a fitness magazine, he comes across two different articles. One article states weightlifting is the best exercise for people due to the continued calorie burn. The other article says aerobics are the best exercise for people based on the calorie burn and cardiovascular aspect of the workout.

Tom views the weightlifting article as absolute truth and posts a copy at the front desk of his gym. At the same time, he disregards the aerobics article and throws it in the trash.

Tom used selective perception to analyze the two articles he read. He accepted the article that supported his beliefs, and he rejected the article that contradicted his thinking.

Emotional status

People interpret and send messages differently based on the emotions they are experiencing. Anger causes people to hear only what they want to hear, depression causes them to shut out others, fear causes them to analyze every word spoken, and nervousness causes them to lose focus of what is being said. Emotional status is a barrier to communication because it influences people's actions and reactions.

Organizational example

Karen and Michelle own a catering company, and they have just had a major disagreement about a business decision. Karen is very upset, when Roger, one of her employees, asks her if he can have the following week off for vacation. Without thinking, Karen immediately tells him he "absolutely cannot have the week off." She then asks him why he would make a "stupid request for vacation" during such a busy time for the caterer.

Karen's emotional status caused her to react more aggressively than necessary to Roger's vacation request. She could have politely asked him if he would consider another week due the heavy work load facing the caterer, but her anger took over and interfered with the intent of her message.

Filtering facts

This occurs when people manipulate or change information so that it is received more favorably. A college student who tells his parents that he rarely consumes alcohol would be filtering facts if in fact he drinks every weekend. This is a barrier to communication because people are not receiving accurate information.

Organizational example

Russell is a maintenance person at a metal fabricator. He is working on the major air compressor at the company and determines that it cannot be repaired. The only solution to this problem is to replace the damaged compressor with a new one.

The new air compressor costs $19,800, but that is not the only expense involved. It also needs be overnighted to the metal fabricator at a cost of $1600. Additionally, it will cost $700 for outside electricians to properly wire it for compliance with electrical code requirements. Finally, an inspection will need to be performed once the compressor is installed, and this will cost $400.

Russell fears giving the owner Linda the bad news about the high cost involved with the new air compressor. He knows money is tight right now, and Linda will likely get upset. However, he also knows that Linda needs to be aware that a new compressor is needed.

Based on the circumstances, Russell decides to manipulate the price so it appears a little less expensive. He tells Linda that the cost of the compressor is going to be about $19,000, and he does not mention the shipping, installation, and inspection costs.

Russell filtered facts in order to avoid upsetting Linda any more than he deemed absolutely necessary. His decision softened the impact of the money needed for the air compressor, but it also distorted the truth about its actual cost.

Information overload

This happens when people have too much information to process in their minds. People experiencing information overload essentially do one of the following:

Ignore information

They ignore all information and simply "walk away" from the matter.

Select information

They reject information that they designate as unimportant in order to pay closer to information that they designate as important.

Forget information

They lose track of information and cannot remember what others have told them.

Information overload is a barrier to communication because people do not process all of the information they receive. This causes important aspects of discussions to be overlooked, ignored, or forgotten.

Organizational example

Elaine is a manager of a group home with 15 teenagers between the ages of 13 and 17. Every kid has experienced problems with the law, and they all come from a troubled past.

Part of Elaine's job involves listening to the teens talk about their problems. Each kid meets with her for two hours per week to discuss issues about family, friends, school, and anything else that comes to mind. This is a good release for the kids, but Elaine simply cannot remember everything they tell her. She takes notes about important aspects of each conversation, but it is too much for her to process all of the information that she receives.

Information overload causes Elaine to consciously select the information she processes for each teenager in the group home. This allows her to retain aspects of the conversations that she finds important, but it also creates potential for missing parts of the conversations that the kids find most significant.

Language differences

As noted in the introduction, jargon and acronyms are examples of how words have different meanings to people. Language differences encompass jargon and acronyms, but they also include everyday words that are not specific to a trade, profession, or industry. For example, a teenager who says a car is "sick" means it is very cool. A fifty-year old adult views the word "sick" in a more negative light.

In short, language is not uniform, and confusion is possible when people think everyone shares a similar perception of the same words. Based on this, one can see that language differences present a barrier to communication.

Organizational example

Doug is a 22-year old college graduate who just started working as a loan officer at a credit union. One of his coworkers, a 40-year old woman named Julie, is talking to him about how she likes using social media to communicate with customers. This interests Doug, and he asks if he can get involved. Julie accepts his request, and they set up a meeting for the next day.

At the meeting, Doug listens intently as Julie discusses credit union customers and social media. However, after about five minutes, he realizes that the term "social media" has a different meaning for him than it does for Julie. Doug views social media as Instagram and Snapchat, while Julies views it as Facebook.

When Doug realizes that Julie is referring to Facebook, he loses interest for getting involved in the social media project. However, he now has no choice since he has already committed.

Language differences caused Doug to misunderstand Julie's interpretation of social media. This communication barrier resulted in him mistakenly committing to something that he had no real interesting in doing.

Nonverbal misunderstanding

This involves actions other than words that lead to confusion. Two subdivisions of nonverbal misunderstanding include written words and nonverbal actions. The following examines each of these in more detail:

Written words

Written communication uses words in a variety of documents including letters, memos, reports, instructions, legal documents, and signs. The information can be handwritten, typed, or professional developed, and it can be composed using word processors, computers, email, texting, tweeting, or instant messaging. Regardless of the method used to compose and display the wording, written communication transfers information to others in writing.

Written words are not understood and interpreted the same way by everyone. They are a barrier to communication because they can create misunderstanding in the workplace.

Organizational example

Charles is a website designer who works at a computer software company. His job affords him the luxury of working full time out of his home office. For the most part, this works out very well for Charles. However, it is challenging at times because the vast majority of his communication is done through email.

Currently, Charles is on a team project with three other employees who physically work at the office. They email back and forth to exchange ideas and information, but sometimes it is hard to understand the true meaning of the messages being sent. For example, Charles sent out an email with some mild sarcasm that was intended to be humorous and harmless, but one of the team members was offended by it. This created unnecessary stress in the group, and productivity came to a halt until it was resolved with series of other emails.

Differences in perception of the email message affected the efficiency of Charles' team. The stress, wasted time, and lack of productivity are indicative that written words can create barriers to communication in the workplace.

Nonverbal actions

This involves virtually every aspect of nonverbal communication that is not written. Body movements, gestures, expressions, positions, and appearance are all part of non-verbal actions. Voice tone, pitch, and quality also fall into this category because they are not spoken words.

People do not always see things the same way, and non-verbal actions can be interpreted differently based on individual perception. They are a barrier to communication because they can create misunderstanding in the workplace.

Organizational example

Ralph is a dry-wall installer at a construction company, and he just received a small pay raise from his boss Yvonne. When she informs him of his raise, he nods his head, smiles politely, and goes back to work.

Yvonne believes Ralph is happy with his pay raise based on his non-verbal actions. Ralph's coworker Lance, however, does not perceive his reaction the same. Lance believes Ralph nodded his head, smiled politely, and went back to work because he was disappointed that he did not receive a bigger raise. If the raise had been bigger, Ralph's reaction would have been more enthusiastic.

This difference in perception could affect the construction company. If Yvonne read Ralph's non-verbal actions correctly, then Ralph will be motivated to work harder. However, if Lance's perception is correct, then Ralph will be demotivated and might start looking for another job. This indicates non-verbal action misunderstanding is a barrier to communication that can potentially have serious consequences.

Gender differences

Men and women have different perceptions of situations, and this can prevent them from effectively working together. Women tend to focus on indirect ways to resolve problems, and they rely on feelings for making decisions. Men often approach problem solving in direct ways, and they rely on facts for decision making. There is no "right" or "wrong" here, but it can create problems in the workplace.

Organizational example

Juanita and are Anthony are engineers employed by a speedboat manufacturer. They are assigned to a team with Mary from the quality department to work on an engine problem that some customers have experienced.

Juanita and Anthony get started on the project, but Mary is unable to attend the first two meetings. She had another work commitment at the time of the first meeting, and she missed the second meeting due to a sick child. This is concerning to Juanita and Anthony, so Juanita suggests they talk to Mary to get a better understanding of her availability for the project. Anthony does not want to meet with Mary. He prefers to kick her off the team and get someone else from the quality department as a replacement.

Juanita does not agree with Anthony about how to handle the situation with Mary. She views his behavior as too aggressive, and she asks her boss if she can be removed from the team based on his actions.

The gender differences in this situation caused a barrier to communication that Juanita did not think could be resolved.   The end result was her asking to be removed from team, and this prevents the team from achieving its objectives.

Cultural differences

Most people who have worked with cultures other than their own understand that the differences can create workplace challenges. These challenges are resolving themselves as organizations become global melting pots, but issues currently exist that negatively influence communication between employees.

Organizational example

Devante' and Carlos are production workers at a food processing plant. Devante' is Black male, and Carlos is Hispanic male. They are both good employees, and have worked their way up to line leaders in the same department.

During company breaks, Devante' sits at a table with all Black employees, and Carlos sits at a different table with all Hispanic employees. This makes the breaks more enjoyable for each man due to commonality factors, but they never converse with each other or discuss ways to make their jobs easier, better, or more efficient.

Essentially, the cultural differences between Devante' and Carlos prevents them leaving their comfort zones and exchanging knowledge.   This hinders the growth of both employees and the food processor, and it shows how cultural differences are a barrier to workplace communication.

Withholding information

Some people intentionally remaining silent in order to withhold information that other employees might find useful. This can cause a variety of workplace problems, and it is often done for job security or power reasons.

Organizational example

Kendall is a CPA at an accounting firm, and she believes that information is power. She does not share any information about her clients with other accountants because she feels she is more valuable to the firm if nobody else has the knowledge that she possesses.

Kendall might have a legitimate point about being more valuable by withholding information, but this is not good for the other accountants or the firm. When she is not at work, other accountants are left in the dark about her clients. They have to call her at home or contact the customer if they need information, and this takes time and effort that would not be required if Kendall shared information.

Kendall's behavior causes problems. Her silence hinders the efficiency of the accounting firm, and it shows how withholding information is a barrier to workplace communication.

Deceitful misrepresentation

This occurs when people purposely do not tell the truth. They manipulate facts, figures, or other information to benefit personally, and their actions cause problems in the workplace.

Organizational example

Paige is a production supervisor at a cell phone manufacturing plant. Her team needs to produce at least 800 phones per shift in order to meet a standard established by corporate management.

On the days that Paige's team does not meet the production standard, she documents equipment breakdowns. These breakdowns did not actually occur, but they are an excuse for the lack of production.

In short, Paige lies when she does not meet her production quota for the day. This makes her look better as a supervisor, but it is also deceitful because the downtime creates issues for the maintenance department. Time is wasted discussing ways to prevent the equipment from breaking down again, and maintenance employees have stress added to their jobs for no reason.

Paige's behavior causes problems. Her lying falsifies records and negatively impacts the maintenance department. It also shows how deceitful misrepresentation is a barrier to workplace communication.

Now you understand some major types of barriers to communication in organizations. In the next section, this discussion will be expanded upon for a more in-depth analysis. In short, major causes of the barriers along with methods for their prevention will be examined.

Causes and Prevention

It's now time to examine the types of barriers to communication discussed above in more detail for better understanding of their workplace significance. Major causes of these barriers and methods for their prevention are as follows:

Selective perception

Causes

Selective perception is caused by confidence, experience in a particular area, or reluctance to change. It involves employees who are not open to anything that contradicts or opposes their beliefs or opinion. This communication barrier results in bias that can be difficult to overcome.

Prevention

One way prevent the bias that results from selective perception is to encourage discussion among employees in all departments. This forces everyone to support their positions after listening to others talk about their ideas for making choices.

Another prevention method involves the distribution of power through checks and balances. If one person has ultimate power, he or she can impede communication using selective perception without being challenged.

Emotional status

Causes

Emotional status is caused by the feelings people are experiencing while communicating. It involves the way emotions affect employees when they send and receive messages. This communication barrier causes people to behave irrationally or illogically in the view of others.

Prevention

People are going to experience negative feelings...and there in no way to stop this from happening. However, the best method for preventing this communication barrier is to postpone discussions with coworkers. Employees who are going through a mentally stressful situation that puts them in a bad mood should avoid discussing important work related matters that might be affected by that mood. Postponement can work wonders because feelings can change drastically over time.

This strategy can also be used for employees who are aware that a coworker is experiencing a troubling emotional state. They should try to reschedule their discussion with the emotionally charged individual...or they might be facing a communication barrier that will be very difficult to overcome.

Filtering facts

Causes

Filtering facts is a result of people wanting to be perceived more favorably by others. In organizations, it often occurs when employees want to appear more competent to their bosses. This communication barrier causes workplace issues because bosses are not receiving accurate information.

Prevention

Employees do not want to appear incompetent or incapable of performing their jobs due to the fear of being ridiculed or punished. For the same reasons, they do not want to admit mistakes...so they filter facts.

One way to prevent employees from filtering facts is to develop a workplace culture that is tolerant of mistakes. This motivates employees to relay accurate information to others, and by doing so it improves communication. One suggestion for accomplishing such a culture is to reward employees who convey accurate information...regardless of whether that information is positive or negative. This reduces the tendency of employees to manipulate facts.

Information overload

Causes

Information overload results when people exceed their capacity to process information. In organizations, this occurs when employee workloads are too much for them to handle. This communication barrier causes workplace problems because information is overlooked, ignored, or forgotten.

Prevention

Employees process a lot of information. That information has an order of importance...and that importance needs to be determined and handled accordingly in order to prevent information overload. This is best done by:

Eliminating email subscriptions

Employees likely do not need all of their email subscriptions. They need to choose the important ones, and unsubscribe from the rest.

Focusing on one topic at a time

This is part of what is often termed "chunking." It involves breaking information into chunks and focusing on one chunk at a time to determine its importance. This reduces information overload because it is easier for employees to process small, rather than large, amounts of information.

Streamlining social media

Social media can be overwhelming because it never ends. Employees likely do not need email, Facebook, Twitter, Snapchat, Instagram, Instant Messaging, and every other form of technological communication they are involved with, so the less important ones need to be eliminated.

Language differences

Causes

Language differences result from language that does not have the same meaning to everyone. In organizations, this occurs when employees do not understand each other's terminology and choice of words. This communication barrier causes confusion and misunderstanding in the workplace.

Prevention

Ways to prevent communication barriers that result from language differences include:

Be specific

Empathy is the key here. Employees need to put themselves in the position of their coworkers when communicating. For example, a 23-year employee needs to be aware that a 62-year old coworker might not be award of newer technology...especially when that technology involves social media.

Ask for clarification

Don't be afraid to ask for help. Employees who don't understand their coworkers' language need to ask for clarification. This might result in minor inconveniences for some people, but it prevents misunderstanding that could be devastating later on.

Use caution with terminology

Terminology is often times very industry specific. Employees who are new to the organization might not have a complete understanding of these terms...especially when they involves acronyms and jargon.

Nonverbal misunderstanding

Written words

Causes

Written word misunderstanding results when people do not clarify the intent of their messages. In organizations, this is most common when employees compose emails. This communication barrier causes misunderstanding, and it can also offend people.

Prevention

The best way to prevent communication barriers that result from written words is to take time to clarify emails and other written documents. Employees should read and reread what they have written to pinpoint areas that could potentially create misunderstanding or offend people. When writing, it is important to remember the old adage, "an ounce of prevention is worth a pound of cure."

Nonverbal actions

Causes

Nonverbal action misunderstanding results from differing interpretations of body movements, gestures, expressions, and positions. In organizations, this communication barrier results from differing employee perceptions.

Prevention

Methods for preventing nonverbal action misunderstanding include:

Control stress

People who are stressed are likely to misread the nonverbal actions of others. Organizations can help employees control stress by offering a discounted gym membership, building a game room, or providing a garden for relaxation.

Control emotions

People who are overly emotional are likely to exhibit nonverbal actions that confuse or alarm others. Organizations can help employees control their emotions by exposing them to emotional intelligence training or webinars.

Gender differences

Causes

Gender differences are the direct result of nature. In organizations, men and women tend to approach work related situations differently. This creates a communication barrier that causes misunderstanding and can be offensive to some employees.

Prevention

Men and women must be able to work together...and this is best done by accepting each other's differences. The best way to learn how to accept each other's differences is to be exposed to diversity training. This training creates tolerance and understanding for those who are different, and it is the key to preventing communication barriers that result from gender differences.

Cultural differences

Causes

Cultural differences result from the environments people live in and the comfort they find within those environments. In organizations, people of different cultures have unique ways of dealing with issues and solving problems. Like gender differences, this creates a communication barrier that causes misunderstanding and offends others. The difference between cultural differences and gender differences is the fact that gender differences can result from people in the same culture.

Prevention

Globalization is changing the demographics of workplaces. People of all cultures are working together, and this means they have to accept and understand each other's differences in order to achieve organizational goals and objectives. Acceptance and understanding can only be achieved when people leave their comfort zones, and this best accomplished through diversity training designed to prevent the communization barriers that result from cultural differences.

Withholding information

Causes

Employees who withhold information generally do it for job security or power purposes. They intentionally remain silent to prevent coworkers from sharing the knowledge that they have acquired. This communication barrier causes workplace problems because it creates unnecessary work and stress for employees who are left in the dark.

Prevention

The best way to prevent communication barriers that result from withholding information is to encourage employee collaboration. This is often done by assigning people to project teams so knowledge is evenly distributed among members.

Additionally, organizations need to establish trust in the workplace to reduce employee fear of sharing information. This is best accomplished by opening the lines of communication between employees and management. The key to open communication is the direct involvement of leadership because this shows employees that the organization is committed.

Deceitful misrepresentation

Causes

Deceitful misrepresentation typically occurs when people do not work hard enough to attain goals or they fail to properly plan for those goals. In organizations, employees manipulate facts, figures, or other information to establish a desired appearance. This communication barrier causes workplace problems because employees on the receiving end are not provided accurate information.

Prevention

The best way to prevent communication barriers that result from deceitful misrepresentation is to establish written rules for dishonesty that include punishment for violation. Organizations can do this very inexpensively, and it can prevent much more costly problems down the line.

Summary

Workplace barriers to communication interfere with messages sent and received by employees. They create misunderstanding that prevents employees from accomplishing the tasks required to achieve the goals of the organization. This misunderstanding can be long-lasting, and the impact can be devastating.

This book focuses on communication barriers in organizations. Specifically, it examines types of communication barriers, causes of communication barriers, and prevention of communication barriers. Simple explanation and related organizational examples are used for better understanding, and this makes learning easy and enjoyable for everyone.

Congratulations! You now understand communication barriers…an important aspect of organizational behavior.

Motivational Theories
Applied to Real World Organizations

Louis Bevoc

Published by
NutriNiche System LLC

Introduction

Motivational theories developed in academic institutions have a lot of value when applied to organizations because they explain employee's behavior. Quite simply, theory and practical application fuel each other in the ever-changing global marketplace.

A concern with these theories, however, is the fact that they are developed in academic institutions under somewhat controlled conditions and environments. In real world organizations, those conditions and environments can vary greatly and make application of the theories questionable.

The book examines the gap between academic theories and real world organizations. Seven major motivational theories are explained, exemplified, applied, and challenged so the reader better understands each of them.

Let's move on to the theories, the people who developed them, and their application to real world organizations.

Theories and Application

Hierarchy of Needs

Description

Psychologist Abraham Maslow developed this theory that proposed the idea that people have needs shaped in a pyramid form. Essentially, basic needs are at the bottom of the pyramid, and they have to be satisfied before moving on to higher level needs.

The five basic needs include:

>*Physiological* (lower order need) – hunger, thirst, shelter, sex, and other bodily needs
>*Safety* (lower order need) – security and protection from physical and emotional harm
>*Social* (higher order need) - affection, belongingness, acceptance, and friendship
>*Esteem* (higher order need) – Internal such as self-respect, autonomy and achievement, and external such as status, recognition and attention
>*Self –actualization* (higher order need) – the drive to become what people are capable of becoming - includes growth, self-fulfillment, and achieving one's potential

Maslow's "needs hierarchy" is arranged so people are motivated to seek satisfaction of the lower level first. Once that level of need has been satisfied, it is no longer a motivator, and the next level of the hierarchy motivates the individual. Basic needs such as shelter, food, and warmth are in at the bottom of the hierarchy. People then progress through physical well-being, social acceptance, self-esteem, and ultimately realize and achieve their potential (self-actualization).

Real world application in an organization

Jeremy is the office manager at an educational research company. He started with the company in data entry nine years ago after graduating from college and gradually worked his way up to managing the entire office staff of 21 employees.

When he first started with the company, Jeremy emphasized the lower order needs. Specifically, he was concerned with pay, health insurance, vacation, and work environment. He wanted to be able to take care of himself financially (physiological needs), and he also wanted some assurance that his employment was stable and secure (safety needs).

After the physiological and safety needs were met, Jeremy looked to coworkers for acceptance and friendship (social needs). He desired interaction with the people in his place of work showed he was looking to fulfill higher order needs. This was accomplished rather easily since Jeremy is friendly and well liked.

After his social needs were satisfied, Jeremy desired to have other higher order needs met. Specifically, he wanted to be recognized and respected (Esteem needs). He took on the office manager's position in order to meet this need.

After working in the office manager's position for several months, Jeremy had one last need he had to satisfy. He desired to become an expert on his job (self-actualization), and did this by attending seminars and working on an MBA.

Limitations

In Maslow's view, people's needs are always changing. Once a need is met, they desire to satisfy another need. In organizations, employee needs change over time and management must adapt to those changes in order to keep them motivated. Sometimes this does not happen, and employees have to move downward within the Hierarchy of Needs.

In the example above, assume Jeremy's health insurance only covers a single person (himself). After he is promoted to office manager and receives his MBA, he marries a woman with a child. He needs have now changed, and he needs health care that provides family coverage instead of single coverage. If his employer does not give him this basic need, he moves back to the lower order and is no longer motivated. He must then make a choice to remain at that level or leave the organization and try again to scale the pyramid at another employer.

Theory X and Theory Y

Description

Douglas McGregor came up with two opposite management views called Theory X (negative) and Theory Y (positive). Theory X represents trusting yourself only to do the right thing. Theory Y represents trusting yourself and your employees.

McGregor's general belief was that we should not have negative pre-conceived notions about human nature. Specifically, he thought managers who believed employees were lazy would make biased decisions, often counterproductive, based on that thinking (Theory X). Theory Y made positive assumptions about people, including the thinking that they would exercise self-direction and assume responsibility if committed to organizational objectives.

Four basic assumptions sum up the premise of each theory. Under Theory X, the following negative assumptions are made:

- Employees dislike work and try to avoid it.
- Employees need to be coerced, controlled, or threatened for task accomplishment.
- Employees elude responsibility and always need direction from supervision.
- Employees are not ambitious and prefer job security over innovation.

Under Theory Y, the following positive assumptions are made:

- Employees like work and look forward to it.
- Employees are self-directed for task accomplishment.
- Employees look for responsibility and are autonomous.
- Employees are creative and seek out novel ways to accomplish goals and expand horizons.

Real world application in an organization

Donna works as a laborer in the packaging department of a bakery. She has worked in this position for the past two years and enjoys her job. Prior to working in packaging, she worked in the cake decorating department. She was not happy in that job and would have left the organization if she was not able to transfer to a different department.

Her current supervisor, Mitch, does not believe in micromanaging. He encourages her to think about changes that could make things more efficient and listens to her suggestions for improvements. His management style promotes responsibility and self-direction, and it encourages Donna to take ownership of her job.

Donna's autonomy and creativity was evident when the packaging department brought in machinery for a new croissant line. She had ideas about where this equipment should be placed for ergonomic and efficiency reasons. Management implemented her thinking, and she won an employee recognition award for her efforts.

Mitch's actions motivated Donna, and he fits the mode of a Theory Y manager.

Donna did not have the same type of supervisor when she worked in the cake decorating department. Her previous boss, Jimmy, always wanted to know what she was doing. He believed in a very rigid protocol and demanded that tasks be performed in a specific manner. If she deterred from his instructions, he threatened her with suspension for insubordination. This management style prevented Donna from taking on responsibility and she did not make decisions without first asking Jimmy.

Donna's fear about decision making was very apparent when management was looking for new cake decorating designs. She did not submit any ideas because she was concerned that Jimmy might feel threatened or become critical. Ultimately, management needed to hire an outside consultant to generate ideas since none of the cake decorators made any suggestions.

Jimmy's actions de-motivated Donna, and he characterizes a Theory X manager.

Limitations

McGregor wanted management to go through another "mental revolution" based on changing negative preconceived notions about employees. He believed the end result of Theory Y would be mutually rewarding for management and workers. However, he also realize after becoming a manager that he could not be popular with everyone and "good human relations" were not a panacea for workplace disagreement. Based on his managerial experiences, McGregor may have agreed that Theory X was somewhat applicable in certain situations.

Let's change the bakery example. Assume Donna is never happy with any decision made. She complains that the employee break room needs to be painted, so management paints it red. She voices her opinion that red was a bad choice, and it should be painted blue. They re-paint it blue, and then she grumbles that they are wasting paint.

On her job, Donna does as little work as possible, never assumes responsibility for completion of a task, files grievances with the union, and constantly tells other employees that the bakery is a terrible place to work. In this case, Donna might need a Theory X manager to list her specific job responsibilities and micromanage her actions.

Goal Setting Theory

Description

This theory was developed by psychologist Edwin Locke, and it is one of the most widely known and respected theories in organizational psychology. Locke's work helped people understand motivation at work and job satisfaction, and it has been applied in a variety of different situations.

In short, Locke thought employees should set difficult and specific goals, and those goals would lead to higher work performance. This theory challenges the idea that employees should simply "do their best" since that type of thinking does not motivate people to perform optimally.

Real world application in an organization

Becky works as loan officer at a major bank. Her job is to entice people to take out mortgages and equity loans through the bank. Typical loan officers at the bank write loans for five to seven new customers per month, but Becky has a goal to sign ten new customers a month for the next year.

She works tirelessly to accomplish her goal, sometimes staying at her desk until 9:00 pm to call customers after they get home from work. Customer response is slow at first, but eventually word-of-mouth spreads that Becky is a great loan officer. Within a few months, people start calling her instead of her calling them.

Over the next year, Becky's hard work pays off as she picks up over 130 new customers. This accomplishment was very challenging, but she was successful because she was motivated by her goal.

The goal was a difficult one, but it inspired her give an effort above and beyond that of the average loan officer.

Limitations

Edwin Locke believed that motivation improves employee performance, and goals provide much of that motivation. This theory is applicable in real world organizations, but it does have some restrictions. For instance, if employee goals differ from that of the organization, then the resulting conflict could cause their job performance to suffer. Additionally, employees can become so obsessed with meeting their goals that they resort to inappropriate or unethical behavior to accomplish them.

In the loan officer example, assume Becky is so focused on meeting her goals that she guarantees customers that their interest rates will go down over time if they use her bank. The bank does not allow loan officers to make this claim because mortgage and equity loan interest rates are based on rates set by the Federal Reserve (Fed). Becky's behavior is unethical and illegal, and it violates bank policy. She makes poor decisions and her performance leads to her termination...all because she had an insatiable desire to meet her goal.

Equity Theory

Description

Behavioral psychologist J. Stacy Adams originated the idea that employees compare their work related contributions and results (inputs) to the same of other employees and make determinations based on what they perceive. In this regard, they are searching for equity between themselves and others in the form of recognition and rewards (outcomes).

The basic thinking behind this is that employees value fair and equitable treatment because it motivates them to perform their jobs to the best of their abilities. Employees who feel under-rewarded or under-compensated will be upset, and they will strive to create a situation that they feel is fair to everyone. Employees who feel over-rewarded or over compensated will also strive for change. The guilt they experience leads them to make an attempt at creating equality in the situation.

The Equity Theory is very useful for measuring job satisfaction. If employees believe their coworkers are being recognized or rewarded more for equal contributions, then they become dissatisfied with their jobs. This theory promotes the thinking that, in order to attain job satisfaction, rewards and recognition (outcomes) must be directly and consistently related to employee contributions (inputs).

Real world application in an organization

An example is Ralph, an assembler at a bicycle shop. Ralph believes he works very hard. In fact, he thinks he is doing much more work than the other two assemblers, and this upsets him because all three employees make the same hourly wage.

Ralph is so bitter that he decides to scale back his work production. He purposely slows down to a pace that he thinks is equal to the other two assemblers. The owner of the shop notices the lack of production, but does not take any action because he cannot afford to give raises, and he needs all three of the assemblers in order to meet his customer demands.

In this particular case, Ralph's response to the perceived "inequity" is a decrease in personal workload and a negative attitude. This response is his attempt to eliminate the inequity, although it does little to resolve the actual problem.

Limitations

People might feel their compensation is equal to others, but this might not motivate them if they think the organization has unfair expectations. Instead, they are bitter at the organization as a whole and this affects their work related contributions.

Assume Ralph believes the other two assemblers are doing an equal amount of work. All three employees assemble two bikes per hour, or 16 bikes in an eight hour shift. However, the owner of the store tells them they need to assemble 25 bikes in an eight hour shift in order to receive a bonus. Ralph realizes that he needs to increase his product by more than fifty percent in order to get a bonus, and that is not possible. In this case, Ralph is not motivated because he views the overall compensation system as unfair.

Expectancy Theory

Psychologist Victor Vroom developed this theory while attempting to come up with a model that showed how people are motivated to make decisions and take action. Essentially, it is based on the thinking that the amount of effort exerted by people on a given task is directly proportional to the rewards they perceive.

Valence, Expectancy, and Instrumentality are the three major factors in this theory that lead to motivation. Valence is the value or importance placed on rewards by employees. This is different for every employee due to the variance in people's perception of value. Expectancy is the belief that employee efforts are directly related to employee performance. In other words, the harder people work, the better they will perform. Instrumentality is the belief that employee performance is directly related to organizational rewards. In simpler terms, better employee performance leads to better rewards.

If all three major three major factors of the theory are not present, then employees fail to become motivated. For example, if they do not believe their efforts are directly related to performance, as is the case in some union environments, then they are not motivated. Additionally, if they do not see increased rewards with increased performance, as in the case of some types of salary or bonus caps, then they lose motivation.

Real world application in an organization

Janet is employed as a salesperson for a book publisher. She works very hard at her job. She spends a lot of time emailing, calling, and personally visiting potential customers in her territory. She is paid straight commission for her sales and likes this structure much better than a salaried position because her earning potential is much higher.

Now let's relate this to the Expectancy Theory. In terms of Valence, Janet places a high value on the rewards (commission dollars) she receives. Her Expectancy is her belief that her hard work contacting customers will result in better performance (more sales). Her Instrumentality is that the increased sales will result in more commission dollars (rewards).

The Expectancy Theory is useful for measuring motivation at work. Motivation is determined by an expected outcome. If that outcome is deemed sufficient, then the employee is motivated to complete the task. The motivation typically depends on the desire of the person to attain the reward, which leads us to the limitations.

Limitations

A major restriction of applying this study in organizations is that employees perceive value differently. It is difficult, if not impossible, for management in organizations to determine a "one size fits all" reward for every employee.

In the book publishing case, management made monetary compensation (commission dollars) the reward. However, assume Janet places a higher value on free time to spend with family and friends. She will not be as motivated as another salesperson who places a very high value on money, so their motivation cannot be measured and compared by the reward alone. Janet might still be motivated to work at the book publisher, but factors outside of the Expectancy Theory play a larger role in her motivation.

Reinforcement Theory

B. F. Skinner, a psychologist and behaviorist, established this theory. It explains people's behavior using the premise that their behavior is transformed by stimuli. In short, people are observed, and their behavior is measured and recorded to establish results.

The Reinforcement Theory is interesting and can be applied to organizational behavior. However, as a whole, it is fairly complicated. A more in-depth analysis, beyond the scope of this book, is needed for the reader to obtain complete understanding. For simplicity purposes, this discussion will focus on increasing desired organizational behavior using positive reinforcement and negative reinforcement, the two primary methods of the theory used for controlling behavior and motivating employees.

Positive reinforcement gives employees things they like when they behave desirably. An example is a supervisor telling an employee that they did a good job after they behave a certain way. The employee is given praise as a reward for his actions, and the idea is that this praise will motivate him to repeat the same behavior.

Negative reinforcement takes away things employees do not like when they behave desirably. For example, a supervisor might be watching an employee very closely while the work. If that employee behaves acceptably, the supervisor stops watching her as closely. The employee was rewarded with autonomy for her actions, and the idea is that this increased freedom will motivate her to repeat the same behavior.

Real world application in an organization

John was recently hired as a custodian in a public high school. Since he has the lowest seniority, one of his responsibilities is cleaning the boys and girls locker rooms. These locker rooms are typically the dirtiest areas in the building, and custodians always complain when they have to clean them.

John has cleaned the locker rooms for three straight weeks without a complaint. The principal of the school notices that the locker rooms have been very clean, and she has not heard any custodians voicing displeasure about performing the task. She inquires about who has been doing the cleaning and finds out it is John. As a form of gratitude, the principal leaves John a hand-written thank you note along with a $20 gift certificate to a local restaurant.

The principal's actions fall within the Reinforcement Theory. Her praise and the gift certificate are rewards designed to motivate John to repeat the same behavior.

Limitations

A major restriction of applying this study in organizations is similar to the issue with the Expectancy theory. Once again, employees perceive value differently and there is no single reward that will equally motivate everyone.

In the custodian example, John might be doing the best job he can because he wants management to reward him by promoting him and giving the task to someone else. The thank you note and gift certificate are nice, but those are not the rewards he is looking to receive. He wants negative reinforcement instead of positive reinforcement.

Another issue with the Reinforcement Theory is the effect of reward tends to diminish over time. The gift certificate and note might have inspired John, but the spontaneity will not be the same the next time he receives them. The principal will need to come up with a different reward because the gift certificate and note lose their motivating appeal over time.

Two-Factor Theory (Motivation-Hygiene Theory)

Psychologist Frederick Herzberg believed people's attitudes toward their jobs could determine their success or failure. Based on this thinking, he tried to figure out what people truly wanted from their employment in terms of job satisfaction. This led him to develop the Two Factor Theory (Hygiene and Motivation Theory). This theory shows that specific job factors are linked to job satisfaction, while other job factors are linked to job dissatisfaction.

Job factors such personal growth, recognition, achievement, and responsibility are linked to job satisfaction because people find them intrinsically rewarding. These factors motivate employees to work longer and harder because they feel like they are important to the organization.

Job factors such as company polices, pay, supervision, and work conditions are linked to job dissatisfaction because people find them extrinsically rewarding. These factors (known as hygiene factors) do not motivate employees to work harder or longer, but they are needed to prevent them from becoming dissatisfied at work.

It should be noted that the elimination of one job factor inked to job dissatisfaction does not bring about job satisfaction. For example, giving an employee a pay raise will not motivate them to be satisfied if they disdain their boss. True motivation, in Herzberg's thinking, can only come from factors linked to job satisfaction.

Real world application in an organization

Shannon is a receptionist at a health club. She is an attractive young lady, and because of this she sometimes gets sexually harassed by certain male customers. These customers tell her how pretty she is and ask her to go out on dates. When she refuses, they continue to pursue her until she makes it very clear that she is not interested.

Shannon is also very good at her job. She goes above and beyond to meet the needs of her customers. The owner realizes her value to the health club, and he gives her a $2000 bonus after only one year in the position. However, the owner does nothing about the occasional sexual harassment, dismissing this as part of the job due to the nature of the clients. This upsets Shannon, and she starts looking elsewhere for employment.

The owner of the health club gave Shannon a raise, but it was not motivating because sexual harassment was still present in the work conditions. This supports the Two-Factor theory by showing that the elimination of one job factor linked to Shannon's job dissatisfaction did not bring her job satisfaction.

Limitations

Herzberg believed intrinsic factors (growth, recognition, achievement and responsibility) are linked to motivation and job satisfaction, while extrinsic factors (company polices, pay, supervision, and work conditions) are not linked to motivation and job satisfaction, but they are necessary to prevent job dissatisfaction. This may be true, but the Two-Factor Theory assumes satisfied workers will be more productive, and this is not always the case. For example, if Shannon chose to satisfy her achievement need by being the top seller of Girl Scout cookies at the health club, then she might be thinking more about selling Girl Scout cookies than doing her job...and she would ultimately be less productive.

Summary

This book focuses on seven major motivational theories. First, the theories are described as they were developed in academia. This shows the original thinking of the creators. Next, the theories are applied to organizations using real world examples. This indicates their usefulness in non-academic settings. Last, but certainly not least, the limitations of the theories are noted. This gives the reader a better understanding of situations where the theories do not apply.

The motivational theories discussed include:

Hierarchy of Needs
Theory X and Theory Y
Goal Setting Theory

Equity Theory
Expectancy Theory
Reinforcement Theory
Two-Factor Theory (Motivation-Hygiene Theory)

You now understand that motivational theories produced in academia are useful in the real world, but they do have limits. This is simply because those theories were mostly developed in academia using interviews, surveys, or controlled subject groups made up of students or paid participants. Real world application was often times not part of the development process, and this is brought to the forefront in certain organizational situations.

Sexual Harassment in Organizations

Causes, Effects, and Prevention

Louis Bevoc

Published by
NutriNiche System LLC

Introduction

What is sexual harassment in organizations? Essentially, it is a type of workplace discrimination based on sex. It can have serious consequences that result in employees feeling insecure and unsafe, and it can affect their ability to earn income. If not controlled, sexual harassment can have devastating effects on employees and employers.

For the purposes of this book, sexual harassment is defined as:

Unwelcome or unwanted sexual comments, advancement, or requests in the workplace

Based on this definition, sexual harassment can be verbal, physical, or psychological...and long as the words or actions are unwelcome and sexual in nature. Additionally, the harasser can be male or female, and same sex employees can harass each other.

Sexual harassment is not the same as harassment; it is a specific type of harassment. In other words, the difference is that all sexual harassment is harassment, but not all harassment is sexual harassment. Another difference is the fact that harassment is tolerated more than sexual harassment. For example, simple teasing of others is rarely considered harassment...but simple teasing of others with sexual innuendoes or references is often considered sexual harassment.

As noted in the preceding paragraph, sexual harassment is a type of harassment. However, this is still a fairly broad category that can include many different types of sexual comments, advancements, or requests in the workplace. To simply the subject matter, specific examples of requests, words, and behavior that fall under sexual harassment are listed below:

Requests

- Asking for sexual favors in return for special treatment
- Asking for sexual favors
- Asking for unwanted dates

Spoken words

- Inappropriate phone calls
- Inappropriate whistling
- Inappropriate howling
- Referring to men or women as hot or babe
- Sexual jokes
- Sexual stories
- Sexual conquests
- Sexual questions
- Sexual comments
- Sexual innuendos
- Questions about sexual preferences
- Questions about sexual history

- Talking about someone else's sex life

Written words

- Inappropriate letters
- Inappropriate emails
- Inappropriate texts
- Inappropriate social media
- Inappropriate faxes

Behavior – no physical contact

- Invading someone's personal space
- Spending excessive time around someone
- Following someone
- Touching oneself sexually
- Sexual gestures
- Winking
- Licking lips
- Blowing kisses
- Staring excessively at someone
- Looking at someone in inappropriate areas
- Cornering a person

Behavior – physical contact

- Sexual assault
- Inappropriate touching
- Unwanted hugs
- Massages

Below is an example of sexual harassment in the workplace:

Nikki works at a doctor's office as a nurse. She is very good at her job, and she is well liked by the staff and patients. One of the physicians, who is also a partner at the practice, has been trying to get Nikki to go out with him for drinks or a night on the town. Unfortunately, Nikki has no interest in this doctor. He is married and much older, and Nikki is simply not attracted to him.

The offending doctor's is persistent about getting Nikki to go out with him. He is not overly aggressive, but his behavior is completely unacceptable. Nikki is not the type to start a lawsuit, but instead chooses to leave the office and take a job as a nurse at a hospital.

The end result of the doctor's sexual harassment was the loss of a good nurse. He was lucky because his practice could have been sued...but Nikki chose to leave the organization rather than take legal action. In short, the doctor's deviant behavior damaged an employee and his practice. Nikki left on bad terms, and the doctor's office lost a good worker.

Now that you have a better understanding of the meaning of sexual harassment, let's move on to some of the reasons that it occurs in workplaces.

Causes

Sexual harassment in organizations is caused by many different factors. All of these factors cannot be discussed in the scope of this book, but some of the major ones include:

- *Culture*

   In some cultures sexual harassment is acceptable. This is especially true in cultures where women are not treated as equals. Harassment typically occurs because an employee from one culture finds something offensive that an employee from another culture finds completely acceptable.

   Cultural sexual harassment is particularly challenging because wrongdoing is often not acknowledged. Perpetrators feel they have a right to behave in a certain manner because their cultural values approve of these actions...and those values can be very difficult to change. Fortunately, the employee being harassed has the law on their side so do not have to tolerate the abuse.

- *Power*

   This is a cause for sexual harassment because perpetrators in power have control over many work aspects of their victims' lives. If those being harassed do not conform or accept the harassment, then their jobs can be made more difficult.

   Men who use power to harass lower level women in the workplace typically do so for the following reasons:

   Humor

   They find women's reactions funny after making sexually explicit comments. The situation is even more amusing if male coworkers are around to see the victim's reaction.

   Earned right

   Their status and position gives them the right to make derogatory or sexually expletive comments. In reality, this is never the case...but some men believe differently.

   Preferential treatment

They offer benefits to certain women in return for sexual favors. For example, they might give the woman an easier job or give them some other type of job related special treatment. This treatment can even include raises and promotions, depending on the extent of the favor.

- ## Self-image

Self-image is the perception each employee has of himself or herself. Contrary to what some people might believe, men and women are sometimes both responsible for self-image issues associated with workplace sexual harassment. Please consider the following as support for the dual responsibility:

Men

Some men see themselves as "playboys" or "studs." They believe women are naturally attracted to them and truly enjoy the attention they receive from sexually explicit behavior or comments. In short, they think their behavior and comments are desired by female employees.

Bear in mind that this only involves a select few men, but the fact is that they do exist...and they can create problems in terms of sexual harassment.

Women

Some women believe that sexual harassment is going to occur in workplaces because "boys will be boy." In other words, men are naturally programmed to make sexually explicit comments or behave in sexually suggestive way. This is the way it was in the past, the way it is now, and the way it will be in the future. In other words, it is part of the culture and needs to be accepted in some form.

Like the egotistical men, these women are also few and far between. However, they do exist in workplaces and they add to sexual harassment problems.

- ## Education

Ignorance of the law does not protect people from being guilty of crime, but lack of understanding is still responsible for some situations involving sexual harassment. This is often due to the fact that some workplaces do not properly educate employees on the subject matter. Uneducated employees are not aware their words or actions are offensive to others, and this causes them to do or say the wrong things. In short, uneducated workforces can lead to sexual harassment issues because employees do not understand what is right and wrong.

- ## Morals

Certain employees do not possess the morals to stop sexually harassing others. They see nothing wrong with their words or actions, and this is why they behave unacceptable.

Unfortunately, perpetrators who lack morals typically feel no remorse for the harm they cause to their sexually harassed victims. They continue to behave wrongly until they are terminated or prevented from doing so by a higher authority.

- *Drugs and alcohol*

Drugs and alcohol cause problems in workplaces all over the world, and sexual harassment is one of those problems. Similar to ignorance, drugs and alcohol are no excuse for sexually harassing coworkers, but they do cause employees to do and say things that they would not do or say if they were sober. In short, drugs and alcohol can lead to sexual harassment issues because employees are not in the right state of mind to act responsibly.

- *Marital situation*

Although it might seem unlikely, marital status can cause employees to sexually harass coworkers. Consider the following situations involving married, divorced, and single employees as support of this statement:

Married

Many people are happily married and sexual harassment is the farthest thing from their minds. However, some marriages become stale or routine...and that presents a problem for certain spouses. Work provides a solution to that problem because the potential for new and exciting relationships exists. Unfortunately, coworkers who are not interested in these unhappily married individuals consider their advancements offensive...and this leads to claims of sexual harassment.

Divorced

Some divorced employees become depressed after the breakup of their marriages. They experience desperation and loneliness, and this makes them reach out to coworkers for intimate relationships. Unfortunately, their coworkers are not always interested in this type of relationship...and it causes problems if the divorced individual is persistent. The situation can get ugly with the end result being an accusation of sexual harassment.

Single

Some single people are unable to differentiate between sexual harassment and flirtation. These cross a line with their advancements toward coworkers, and this leads to situations that typically end up bad.

- *Opportunity*

Some employees believe in the saying, "when opportunity knocks, be ready to open the door." This is good advice for many work related situations, but it is greatly exaggerated in others...especially those with the potential for sexual harassment. For example, people who work alone in their office late at night are not necessarily looking for an intimate relationship with a coworker. Along the same lines, taking a business trip with a coworker does not guarantee a sexual liaison. Unfortunately, some employees believe there is opportunity for intimacy in situations such as these, and they try to take advantage that opportunity. Not surprisingly, the end result is often an accusation of sexual harassment.

Now you understand some of the major causes associated with sexual harassment in organizations. These are important for understanding why this illegal activity is a concern in so many workplaces. That being said, let's move into in the next section that examines the effects of sexual harassment on employees and employers.

Effects

- *Turnover*

    Sexual harassment can result in employees leaving organizations. These employees can include the harasser, the victim, or other workers. The following are explanations of why this turnover occurs:

    Harasser

    Perpetrators who are accused or found guilty of sexual harassment often leave workplaces out of shame or anger. The might be ashamed because they are embarrassed of their behavior, or they might be angry because they believe they did nothing wrong. Either way, they leave the organization because they do not want to continue working for their current employer.

    Another reason for harasser turnover is termination. Those accused of sexual harassment are terminated by their employer after a review of their actions. This wrongful behavior is considered so serious that some organizations have zero tolerance policies in place that result in immediate termination.

    Victim

    Unfortunately, victims of sexual harassment also leave organizations. Some of these employees refuse go back to the place where they were subjected to the wrongful behavior, and others are not capable of returning due to the hurt they suffered. In cases involving lawsuits, some settlements stipulate that the employees never return to the organizations where they were sexually harassed.

    Other workers

    Workplaces that experience severe cases of sexual harassment can drive out employees who were not victims or perpetrators. They decide that they do not want to be employed in an environment where this type of behavior occurs, and they leave the organization. This is a good example of the impact that sexual harassment can have on entire workforces.

- *Promotions*

  In some situations, management views employees who complain about sexual harassment as "troublemakers" who are not good for the organization. These employees are then black-listed and prevented from being promoted or moving into better positions. Fortunately, this is not the norm in most workplaces...but it does occur, and it can put employees in positions that stop them from progressing in their careers.

- *Fear*

  Victims of sexual harassment often experience fear because they are afraid of the perpetrator. This effect can be one of the most devastating because it is not limited to the workplace. It can also occur while the victim is at home or outside the house....so the fear never goes away. As might be expected, work productivity diminishes for individuals living in constant fear.

- *Motivation*

  This effect is very common. Victims of sexual harassment often lose their motivation at work...especially if they believe management did not do enough to stop the wrongful behavior and rectify the situation. Lack of motivation results in lower job performance, and this hurts the employee and the employer.

- *Trust*

  Trust is critical in organizations, and it erodes quickly when employees are sexually harassed. Workers need to feel they are safe in a workplace, and sexual harassment creates a feeling that is the exact opposite. The worst part about this effect is that once trust is lost, it is very difficult to restore.

- *Absenteeism*

  As noted several times in this book, sexual harassment is a serious issue. It can lead to victims becoming depressed, and depression can lead to absenteeism. When employees are absent, their jobs suffer...and this impacts the bottom lines of organizations.

- *Lawsuits*

  This effect negatively influences organizations. Lawsuits impact the reputations of organizations, require time, and cost money. Regardless of the outcome, organizations lose in one way or another.

- *Costs*

Many costs are associated with sexual harassment. There is a cost of turnover when good employees are lost and need to be replaced, there is a cost of promotions when good employees are passed over, there is a cost of fear, motivation, trust, and absenteeism when productivity is lowered, and there a cost of reputation, time, and money when lawsuits emerge. The costs associated with sexual harassment can devastate workplaces...and in severe cases they can stop organizations from functioning.

Now you are aware of some of the major negative effects of sexual harassment in workplaces. These effects present many problems for employees and employers, and they can destroy organizations that do nothing stop them.

This leads to a question. What can be done to prevent sexual harassment in workplaces? This answer involves the incorporation of several different methods that require time, effort, and money...and they are all discussed in the next section.

Prevention

It is rather obvious that sexual harassment cause problems in organizations. That being said, it needs to be prevented, and the following are some methods of prevention:

- *Education*

    Training is likely the most time consuming and expensive method...but it pays off in the long run. Employees need to be educated about sexual harassment so they clearly understand wrong behavior from right behavior, and this is best done using workforce training.

    In the United States, certain states require sexual harassment training, but others do not. Regardless of the requirements, all states encourage sexual harassment training because laws make it illegal.

    Training should start at orientation and be part of an ongoing process. It should also be two-fold, focusing on employees and supervision. Specific types of training include:

    Orientation training

    This type of training starts as soon as an employee is hired. The goal of orientation training is to immediately establish acceptable and unacceptable employee behavior.

    In terms of sexual harassment, orientation training makes workers aware of the rules that are in place and the fact that employees are expected to follow them.

    Employee training

    Employees must be made aware that they there is no tolerance for sexual harassment. Any violations will be dealt with swiftly, and the punishment might include termination from the organization.

Employees must also be encouraged to report sexual harassment that they witness to supervisors. They need to know that their reporting will be taken seriously and kept in complete confidence.

In short, the most important aspects of employee training are to (1) establish sexual harassment rules with consequences for violation and (2) build trust that management will react appropriately to any report of a coworker being sexually harassed.

Supervisor training

Supervisors need to understand that part of their jobs involves keeping employees happy. Happy employees find satisfaction with their jobs, and they are less likely to sexually harass a coworker.

Supervisors also need to be trained to listen to employee concerns and act accordingly. Their involvement is a key to stopping sexual harassment from occurring.

- ## Hiring practices

This is the most important prevention method because, if done correctly, it stops problem people from becoming employees.

Every employer should conduct background checks on people before hiring them. These checks can find out a lot of information about individuals...including their history of sexual harassment at previous jobs. Three major checks related to sexual harassment include:

Criminal history

This is the most common and obvious check. It indicates past sexual harassment issues, and it also shows any type of problematic behavior that might be related.

Employer history

This indicates things an employee might have done that might not be part of their criminal history. For obvious reasons, past sexual harassment is not something that most people would willingly divulge.

Academic history

Academic history is important because sexual harassment discovered by universities or colleges is often a permanent part of a student's file. Again, this is something that might not be a part of their criminal history.

- ## Company policies

This is the easiest method of prevention because any organization can implement policies. Policies set a clear tone of what is expected of employees. They promote positive behavior, discourage any type of sexual harassment, and outline discipline protocols for violating established rules.

These polices must be written, and the best way to introduce them is during employee training or meetings. Employee signatures indicate they understand the rules involving sexual harassment, and signatures are difficult to dispute when problems occur. This assures management that discipline can be taken without fear of future legal action.

- *Human resources*

Some employees are not comfortable discussing sexual harassment problems with their boss or other managers in the organization. These employees often turn to human resources for their concerns.

One important point to remember here is employees who report sexual harassment issues to human resources must have trust that their discussions will be kept in confidence. If they do not have trust, then they will not expose problems.

- *Management involvement*

Management needs to be committed to sexual harassment by actively encouraging employees to point out problems. If leaders do not prioritize sexual harassment prevention, then employees will not sense seriousness and will not come forward with problems they observe.

In order to effectively be involved, management needs to:

Monitor the workplace

Managers need to continue walk around the organization and ask employees about their perceptions of the workplace environment. This action will entice employees to talk if they are witnessing coworkers who are sexually harassing others or are being sexually harassed.

Encourage employee involvement

Managers must encourage employees to come forward when they witness any type of sexual harassment. This can be done through personal meetings, phone calls, emails, or anonymous notes.

Employees also need to know that there is an open door policy regarding sexual harassment. They are always welcome to inform management of problems so management can appropriately react.

Take swift action

Managers who are made aware of a sexual harassment issue need to act swiftly to stop it and prevent a future reoccurrence. This shows that they support their employees, and they want the workplace to be free of this wrongful behavior.

Summary

Sexual harassment is unwelcome or unwanted sexual comments, advancement, or requests in the workplace. It can be verbal, physical, or psychological. Harassers can be male or female, and same sex employees can harass each other.

This book focuses on sexual harassment in organizations. First, it looks at causes including culture, power, self-image, education, morals, drugs and alcohol, marital situation, and opportunity. Next it examines effects including turnover, promotions, fear, motivation, trust, absenteeism, lawsuits, and costs. Finally it suggests ideas for prevention including education, hiring practices, company policies, human resources, and management involvement. The text is written with simple explanations for easy reader understanding and comprehension.

Congratulations! You now have a better understanding of sexual harassment in workplaces...an important aspect of organizational behavior.

Absenteeism
in Organizations
Causes, Effects, and Prevention

Louis Bevoc

Published by
NutriNiche System LLC

Summary   57

Introduction

Absenteeism is employees' unscheduled absence from their jobs. The key word here is "unscheduled." Scheduled absences can be planned for in advance, and this helps avoid some of the potential problems that might occur during the employees' time off. However, there is very little time to plan for unscheduled absences, and the necessary resources might not be available on a moment's notice.

Leaders in organizations are not naive enough to think employees are going to be at work on every scheduled day. They expect workers to miss some time because they are not feeling well or want to attend to personal matters that conflict with the times they are supposed to be at work. This is acceptable and does not present a problem...unless it becomes excessive.

When absenteeism becomes excessive, it is a major headache for organizations. If employees do not show up for work, then their jobs need to be performed by someone else. If no one else is available, then those jobs simply do not get done. This creates difficult and stressful situations for workers and managers, and it occurs far too often in some workplaces.

Absenteeism has a greater impact on smaller organizations than it does on larger ones due to the size of the workforces. For example, a business with 100 employees will function close to normal if five people are absent. However, a business with eight employees might operate if five workers are missing.

Regardless of the number of employees in a workplace, excessive absenteeism causes problems. It stresses out the employees who are forced to take on additional workloads, lowers morale, and affects productivity. Ultimately, it impacts the financial well-being of organizations as they struggle to meet the needs of their customers.

Since there are problems associated with absenteeism, leaders of organizations need to do whatever they can to minimize it. This starts by gaining a better understanding of the causes and effects.

This book examines the causes and effects of absenteeism. It explores the reasons employees miss scheduled days of work and analyzes the problems this causes for organizations. It also offers suggestions for preventing workplace absenteeism so the negative effects can be minimized.

Now that you have a basic understanding of workplace absenteeism and the scope of this book, let's move on to the discussing the causes of this problem.

Causes

As noted in the introduction, absenteeism is employees' unscheduled absence from their jobs. Unscheduled absence can be intentional or unintentional as shown in the following examples:

Intentional absenteeism

Manny comes home from work on Wednesday night and finds an envelope in his front door. As a surprise, one of his best friends leaves two baseball tickets to the Atlanta Braves home opening game that starts Thursday at noon. Manny is thrilled, and he texts his friend that he will be at the game.

The next morning, Manny calls his employer and tells them that he will not be in to work. He says he has some "personal business" that he needs to attend to, and he will return on Friday.

Manny's decision to miss work in order to go to the baseball game is an example of intentional absenteeism.

Unintentional absenteeism

Juanita and George are married with two children under the age of five. They both work full time jobs, and her husband frequently travels. This week he is away on a business trip.

George's business trips are normally not a problem for Juanita because drops her children off at day care in the morning before going into work. However, this morning she wakes up to find her daughter vomiting. This child will not be able to go to day care today and Juanita is the only person who can care for her. She calls work and tells them that she will not be in today due to a sick child.

Juanita's decision to miss work in order to take care of a sick child is an example unintentional absenteeism.

In the view of an employer, Juanita's decision is much more legitimate than Manny's for missing work. However, regardless of the intent, unscheduled absences do not allow organizations to plan for handling missing employee's work that needs to be completed. For this reason, it is important to understand the causes of absenteeism so attempts can be made to eliminate them and minimize absences on scheduled work days.

It is virtually impossible to list every cause of absenteeism due to the fact that every employee is unique. However, the following are some major causes of these unscheduled absences:

Stress

Work related stress can lead to mental and physical health problems if it is not dealt with in some manner. Employees use a variety of different techniques to deal with stress including yoga, exercise, meditation, relaxation, massage, and therapy. However, workers also deal with stress by not showing up for work...and this is why it is a cause of absenteeism.

Family care

Family care has changed considerably since the 1960s. Mothers used to stay home to take care of children while fathers worked to financially support the family. However, this has changed. Today many, if not most mothers, are employed in some capacity. Children go to day care and are picked up after the parent's workdays are finished.

The dual income family works well financially for many families, but this arrangement poses a problem when children get sick. One of the parents needs to stay home to care for the child, and this means that he or she needs to miss work. Although this absence is unintentional, it is still unscheduled and therefore classified as absenteeism.

Family care absenteeism does not end with care for children. Employees today are part of the "sandwich generation" where they need to help young children and aging parents. When a parent needs assistance, one of their children needs to miss work to provide the necessary care...and the end result is an unscheduled absence. So, the same people who miss work for their children can also miss work for their parents.

In short, family care today is major cause of absenteeism based on dual income households and the needs of various relatives. This will continue to present a challenge as long as working couples have young children and aging parents.

Bereavement

An old saying goes, "two things people have to do during life are die and pay taxes." The taxes part is debatable...but the part about dying is an absolute fact.

When people die, friends and family need time to grieve over the loss. However, it is difficult to specify how long employees should mourn because everyone is different. Some workers need more time than others, and therefore end up missing more days of work. Since this missed time is unscheduled, it is considered absenteeism.

Illness

Essentially, illness can be physical or mental. Physical illness can be as simple as the common cold or as serious as terminal cancer. Mental illness often involves some type of depression, but it can also involve issues such as paranoia or schizophrenia.

The following examines the two types of illness in more detail:

Physical illness

It is not uncommon for employees to become physically ill. Their illnesses often require them to miss work, and the number of days they are absent depends on the time required for healing.

Management expects employees to miss some time at work due to physical illness, but that time is not scheduled in advance and is therefore deemed absenteeism.

Mental illness

Mental illness is not as common as physical illness, but it does affect employees in every type of workplace. This illness often requires people to miss work, and they are not able to return until their conditions are cured or controlled.

Management typically does not expect employees to miss work due to mental illness, but they do understand that it does occur. However, the time missed is unscheduled and is therefore considered absenteeism.

Bullying

Employees who are bullied by coworkers might choose stay home rather than come to work and take the abuse. This type of situation is unfortunate because bullying can lead to depression and long-term negative effects. Bullying might not be one of the most common causes of absenteeism, but it is one of the most important due to other problems that can result.

Poor supervision

Poor supervision is a problem in many organizations, but only the more severe cases result in absenteeism. Employees simply cannot bear to see their supervisors, so they decide to call in sick. They become overwhelmed with negative thoughts, and choose to avoid the situation rather than deal with bosses that they disdain.

Workload

Workloads can be so excessive that employees choose to stay home rather than go to work. Ironically, the absenteeism resulting from workloads is often an indirect consequence of other absenteeism. This is because employees miss work and their coworkers have to do their jobs. Those coworkers then have much larger workloads, so they also decide to not show up for work. Unfortunately, this cycle can repeat itself until the overworked employees burn out and permanently leave the organization.

Working conditions

Working conditions have a big impact on absenteeism. Workplace temperature, sanitary conditions, and ergonomics all play role in determining if employees will show up for work. Please consider the following examples:

Cold temperatures (workplace temperature)

Cold temperatures create discomfort and causes workers to lose focus. All they think about is getting to a warmer environment, and that in itself is enough to make them not show up for work.

Dirty workplaces (sanitary conditions)

Unsanitary conditions result in mental disgust for some employees. They would rather be home than in a dirty workplace and decide not to come to work.

Poor lighting (ergonomics)

Dimly lit areas cause eye strain. This makes it difficult to complete work, and causes headaches. Due to the pain, employees call in sick.

Travel

Some jobs require employees to travel. This is not a problem unless the travel becomes excessive. Employees do not want to constantly be on the road because they miss out on many aspects of their personal lives. When they finally get home, they want to spend time with family and friends rather than going right into the office...so they tell their employer that they will not be in. This is understandable, even in the eyes of some employers, but it is still considered absenteeism.

Personal reasons

There are times when people do not go to work for personal reasons. They choose to attend a daytime sporting event, catch a matinee movie, go on a day trip with a friend, or just relax in front of the television at home. This is also known as "playing hooky," and it happens in workplaces all over the world.

Employers typically do not view personal reasons as legitimate excuses for missing work. However, they realize that employees are going to "play hooky," and there is not much that can be done about it.   This form of absenteeism will likely occur in some capacity as long as people work for organizations.

Injury

Injuries are legitimate reasons for missing work. When employees are hurt, they cannot perform certain aspects of their jobs, and therefore need to be off work.

As far as employers are concerned, there two basic types of injuries including:

Work related

These injuries result from accidents that occur on the job. Workers' compensation pays for the employees' time missed because the injury occurred while working. This is bad for the employer for two different reasons because (1) their insurance premiums increase due to the claims and (2) their employees are not able to perform their jobs.

Non-work related

These injuries result from accidents that do not occur on the job. Employers are not required by law to compensate employees who are not injured at work...although some provide short-term and long-term disability benefits. Employers save money by not paying injured employees, but they still lose because these individuals are not able to perform their jobs.

Employers realize that injuries are going to occur. However, these claims can be abused. Workers who do not want to come back to work can often get doctors to extend their excused absence regardless of the whether or not they are healed. If this happens, then absenteeism is even more costly to employers...especially if workers compensation is being paid to the injured employees.

Other employment

Some employees miss work because they are working other jobs. This is usually not acceptable to employers...and some even consider it grounds for termination. However, regardless of the rules in place, other employment is a cause of absenteeism that occurs in many workplaces.

Job searches

This involves missing work to (1) look for another job or (2) interview at another organization. Obviously, most employers would frown upon this because they are on the verge of losing employees...and those employees might be going to competitors. However, in reality, missing work for job searching is fairly common because interviews are typically conducted during normal working hours.

Transportation

Most people need some type of transportation to get to their jobs. If that transportation is not available, then they are unable to show up for work. This type of problem is more common for employees who rely on public transportation, but personal vehicles also break down.

Transportation issues are usually beyond the control of employees. However, they are still considered unscheduled absences and a cause of absenteeism.

Excessive hours

Employees who work too many hours sometimes miss work just to get some personal time away from the job. For example, a production plant might be working seven days a week. After two or three weeks without a day off, employees decide to stay home and rest instead of going into work. This rest is obviously justified, but it is considered absenteeism.

Strange hours

Some employees miss work because they work strange shifts or hours. For example, third shift employees might never get to see their families or friends, so they decide to not come into work in order to attend special events in their lives. This type of absenteeism it is more likely to happen to employees who work when most people are at home or out socializing.

Religion

Leaders in organizations are beginning to realize that employees need time off for designated religious occasions that might not be recognized by the government. However, this type of management thinking is in its infancy, and it will be a while before employees are excused for the days they consider sacred. Until that time, workers will not show up for work for religious reasons, and their unscheduled absences will be considered absenteeism.

Drugs and alcohol

Substance abuse is an issue in many workplaces, and this is likely to continue as long as drugs and alcohol are readily available to employees. In some cases, management is required by law to allow employees time to deal with their addictions...and these absences are not part of absenteeism since they are scheduled. However, hangovers and other substance related aftermath are considered absenteeism, and they will likely never be accepted as legitimate by leaders of organizations.

Attitude

Attitude is a major cause of absenteeism. Employees who have negative attitudes about their place of work tend to show up less frequently than coworkers with positive attitudes. Attitude is about perception...and perception truly is reality.

Age

Age is also a cause of absenteeism. Typically, younger workers miss time because they are out socializing or having fun. Older employees often miss time for health concerns or family situations.

Younger and older employees miss work for different reasons, but all of those reasons result in unscheduled absences.

Seniority

Long-term employees sometimes feel a sense of entitlement when in terms of taking unscheduled time off from work. They have been with the organization for a long time and believe their seniority gives them the right to be absent without notice. Unfortunately, this is still considered absenteeism...and it requires other employees to do extra work.

Boredom

Repetition makes jobs mundane. Employees lose the motivation to work after repeating the same task throughout their work day, and this leads them to take unscheduled days off work. In short, boredom is a cause of absenteeism because it does not provide employees with challenges.

Some causes of absenteeism are specific to certain groups of employees such as immigrants. These include:

Family businesses

Some employees miss work because they need to work at seasonal family businesses. For example, they might need to leave to help their family work the fields during harvesting periods.

Absenteeism caused by family businesses can be a big problem for organizations if too many workers leave at the same time. Mass exodus of employees can cripple productivity and even force some organizations to cease operations.

Unrecognized holidays

Similar to religious occasions, some holidays are not recognized by organizations in the United States. Examples include Cinco de Mayo, Greek Easter, and Rosh Hashanah.

Management is beginning to realize that employees need time off for designated holidays, but it will be a while before they are formally excused. Until that time, workers will not show up for work on days they consider holidays, and their unscheduled absences will be considered absenteeism.

Homeland visits

Some employees miss work because they go back to their homelands to visit friends and family. These visits are very important to these workers, and they leave regardless of whether their absences are approved by management.

This type of absenteeism is difficult to prevent because employees have strong ties to people from their countries of origin.

Now you understand some of the major causes of absenteeism, and this is important in order to develop methods of prevention. However, before exploring ways to prevent absenteeism, the effects that it has on workplaces needs to be examined.

Effects

Absenteeism negatively affects employers and employees in a variety of different ways. Some of the major ways include:

Costs

There are high costs associated with absenteeism. Some of these costs are:

Wages and benefits

In many cases, especially those involving worker's compensation, absent employees still receive wages and benefits until they are able to return to work. In some cases, these payouts can go on for years...and possibly even the rest of the employees' lives.

Overtime

As noted earlier, absent employees leave work behind that still needs to be done by coworkers. Those coworkers need to work longer hours to complete the designated tasks, and they are paid overtime for those hours.

Training

Absent workers sometimes need to be replaced by new employees. These new employees need to be trained...and that training has a cost associated with it.

Administrative

Many people are not aware that there are administrative costs for managing absenteeism. For short-term absences, letters need to be sent to the offenders detailing disciplinary action. For long-term absences such as those involving workers' compensation, massive amounts of paperwork need to be filled out...and this takes time and resources. Additionally, meetings need to be conducted with insurance companies, medical providers, and attorneys to discuss specifics of the case.

In short, absenteeism impacts the bottom lines of organizations. This impact is never good, and it can lead to some companies permanently shutting down.

Productivity

Absenteeism results in decreased productivity. This is due to the fact that experienced employees are missing from the workplace, and coworkers who are less familiar with their jobs need to fill in.

Morale

When employees are forced to take on more work due absenteeism, they often become frustrated with their jobs. They resent management for the increased workload, and their morale decreases.

Trust

When employees are forced to take on more work due absenteeism, they lose trust in management. The absenteeism is not their fault, yet they are paying the price. The worst part about issues involving trust is the fact that it is very difficult to restore once it is lost.

Stress

When employees are forced to take on more work due absenteeism, they experience job stress. Over time, this causes them to burnout...and burnout causes their absenteeism to increase. It is rather ironic, but absenteeism results in absenteeism.

Turnover

When employees are forced to take on more work due absenteeism, they start to dislike their jobs. This causes them to leave their organizations for other positions. In short, absenteeism results in turnover.

Now that you understand some of the more important effects of absenteeism, it is time to move into the next section that discusses methods of prevention.

Prevention

Once absenteeism starts, it can snowball and quickly get out of control. This is why the best way to stop it is to prevent it from occurring.

Some of the best methods of prevention include:

Hiring practices

Effective hiring practices are likely the best way to prevent absenteeism because (1) they prevent problem employees from entering the workplace and (2) they prevent employees from becoming problem employees.

The following are some important aspects of effective hiring practices:

Check references

It's always a good idea to call past employers to determine if potential employees have a history of absenteeism. It is illegal for employers to divulge certain facts about past employees, but they can release attendance records if policies were in place. This allows organizations to find out if potential employees were terminated for absenteeism related reasons.

Emphasize attendance importance

The importance of showing up for work should be stressed at the time of hiring. This makes it clear to employees that they are needed on the job and expected to show up when they are scheduled.

Orientation training

This occurs after the employee is hired. Orientation training talks about absenteeism and details the attendance policies in place...including disciplinary actions for violations. Training can be expensive, but it is well worth the cost if it is properly conducted.

Rewards

Rewards are a good way to prevent absenteeism because they provide goals and motivation for employees to show up for work.

There are several different types of rewards including:

Awards

Awards are typically certificates that commend good employee attendance. They are motivational because employees are recognized in front of the entire organization. They can also be used by employees for negotiating raises and other perks at a later time.

Incentive pay

This involves paying employees for good attendance. In other words, the incentive for reducing absenteeism is a cash reward. Typically, these are paid out on a monthly basis, and they can be in the form of an annual or bi-annual bonus.

Paid time off

Some organizations reward employees for good attendance by giving them paid time off. Certain workers prefer this over cash incentives because they value time more than additional income.

Lotteries

This involves lotteries for workers with good attendance. These individuals are entered in periodic (often monthly) lotteries with cash prizes that go to the selected winners.

All of the above rewards can be based on attendance systems put in place by organizations. For example, a system that issues employees points for unscheduled or unexcused absences could be utilized. Employees who reach a specified number of points are progressively disciplined...up to the point where they are terminated for extreme absenteeism.

Rewards can also be used to create peer pressure. Team or organization wide absenteeism systems can be put in place that document employee absenteeism as a whole. This results in employees monitoring each other's attendance because one employee's absenteeism can prevent everyone from receiving rewards.

Job rotation

This prevents absenteeism by (2) reducing the boredom of performing only one job and (2) empowering employees because they are more involved in the operation of the organization.

Another benefit is the fact employees know each other's jobs when someone is absent. This reduces mistakes and saves time in terms of training.

In short, job rotation reduces absenteeism because employees want to come to work, and they understand each other's jobs.

Communication

If absenteeism is an issue, management should ask employees why it is occurring. They might be surprised with the answers they receive from workers, and those answers can be used to prevent reoccurrences.

For example, some employees might indicate that they are missing time because other employees are always absent... and management does nothing about it. If this is the case, then an attendance system needs to be implemented.

As the saying goes, "a little communication goes a long way."

Summary

Absenteeism is employees' unscheduled absence from their jobs. Leaders of organizations generally do not have a problem with absenteeism unless it becomes excessive. Excessive absenteeism creates headaches for organizations because job tasks still need to be completed with fewer employees.

This book examines the causes and effects of absenteeism. It explores the reasons employees miss scheduled days of work, and it analyzes the problems this causes for organizations. It also offers suggestions for preventing workplace absenteeism so the negative effects can be minimized. Simple explanations are used for easy reader comprehension and understanding.

Congratulations! You now understand more about workplace absenteeism...and important aspect of organizational behavior.